A JOURNEY TO
Deliverance And Healing

Dr. Sheila Marie Brockett

PATASKITY PUBLISHING CO.

Pataskity Publishing Co.

207 Hudson Terrance Suite 102

Augusta, GA 30906

pataskitypublishing.com

(706) 250-3956

Copyright © 2021 Dr. Sheila Marie Brockett.

All rights reserved.

No portion of this book may be reproduced mechanically, electronically, or by any other means, including photocopying, without the author's written permission. It is illegal to copy this book, post it on a website, or distribute it by any other means without permission from the author.

Dedication

I dedicate this book to the loving memory of my mother,
Teresa Ellen Linen-Holmes.

Acknowledgement

My loving husband, you never cease to share your admiration, praise and support. Thank you, Peter Irwin Brockett, for being an ongoing reminder of God's grace in my life.

To my three daughters, **Aviyon Sabb, Shaquana Sabb, Shiamonte Sabb**, thank you for your love and support and for being a driving force to help me complete seminary.

To my father, **Delman Holmes**. I appreciate my upbringing and for being a great father. I will always have memories of you being a good father.

Thanks for the great men and women of God who impacted my life. The healing and deliverance services that I attended, the prayer groups that I sat in as a long-term student of the Gospel of Jesus Christ. The molding and shaping me to complete his finished work in me. Thank you for great pastors, prophets and teachers and prayer that impacted my life.

Table of Contents

Table of Contents
About The Author 1
Abstract 3

Chapter 1 — 9
Strongholds 9
Abnormal Behavior 9

Chapter 2 — 17
Recognizing Victories In Jesus Christ 17
Curses 17

Chapter 3 — 28
Identifying Drug And Alcohol Abuse Deliverance From Drug And Alcohol Abuse 28

Chapter 4 — 34
Identifying Lust 34
Deliverance From Lust 34

Chapter 5 — 38
Identifying Slothfulness 38
Deliverance From Slothfulness 38

Chapter 6 — 44
Identifying Generational Curses 44
Deliverance From Generational Curses 44

Chapter 7 — 49
The Power Of God's Word 49
Healing Power 49

Chapter 8 — 54
How To Dismiss Addiction & Stronghold — 54
Confess Your Sin — 54

Chapter 9 — 58
Personal Deliverance & Victory — 58
Examples Of Spirits — 58

Chapter 10 — 63
Scriptures Of Deliverance & Healing The Power Of Fasting And Prayer — 63

About The Author

Dr. Sheila M. Brockett (Dr. Brockett) is married to Pete Irwin Brockett. She currently resides in Myrtle Beach, South Carolina. Dr. Brockett has been in ministry since her early twenties, and continues to work in various areas of ministry. She also furthered her education at Horry Georgetown Technical College, Ashworth University, Iap College and Zion Bible Institute. Dr. Brockett not only enjoys teaching and flowing in the prophetic anointing, but also being an entrepreneur, and coaching people to a better life. She is a certified life coach and motivational speaker. She has a Doctoral of Religion and Masters of Theology, and she is a board-certified activity professional. She has an Associate in Human Resource Management. Dr. Brockett's experiences in ministry have opened doors, and provided a lot of opportunities. She is a Certified Wedding Planner, a notary, and part of the American

Marriage Ministry (AMM). Dr. Brockett marries couples after providing counseling services. She is an ordained minister of Grace Fellowship International Network. She has experienced counseling different people. Her experiences ignited the desire in her to become a Life Coach, and most of all to help those in need of counseling. Isaiah 9:6 states, "For unto us a child is born, unto us a son is given: and the government shall be upon his shoulder: and his name shall be called Wonderful, Counsellor, The mighty God, The everlasting Father, The Prince of Peace."

Abstract

Psychology is very humanistic in all of its forms. Psychology teaches that one's behavior can be eradicated with self- help programs which are inspired by man's philosophy. In my personal experiences, I have recognized that people who lack experiences of certain struggles may not be the most appropriate psychologist for people experiencing challenges in those specific areas. For example, you may wonder *"How can a non-alcoholic person teach someone to be set free, or stop drinking and abusing alcohol? How can someone who has never consumed drugs help a drug addict become free?"* Humanism teaches us that the power to be healed is in you as it rests in you. Humanism teaches that you are a god. Various addictions are sicknesses and unclean habits that can be inherited, involved, or voluntarily fabricated. These addictions initially begin as an enjoyment; however, the addictions will progress to become a destructive habit.

The purpose of this book is to teach anyone who may read this book being a believer or unbeliever that deliverance is available. We do not have to live with strongholds. I have experienced Christian people struggling with popping pills because they are in pain. I have witnessed people resorting to various solutions while failing to make a connection with the monotheistic God as he is the answer to all of our life's problems. I want people to know that Jesus Christ is the answer to any challenges that we are faced with. For example, Jesus states in John 15:1-3, "I am the true vine, and my Father is the husbandman. Every branch in me that beareth not fruit he taketh away: and every branch that beareth fruit, he purgeth it, that it may bring forth more fruit. Now, ye are clean through the word which I have spoken unto you." This scripture allows us to know that we can be cleansed of any ungodliness as we are cleansed through God's Word.

Once I completed three months dealing with people of certain addictions, I realized that certain spirits caused more spirits, and certain spirits are attached to certain addictions. If you *clean your house up* and get rid of these spirits, but return to the same behaviors, these spirits come back. They are coming back more powerful. We have to be on guard all the time as Christians. We are living in a time of deception. The Bible warned us of these times as 1st Timothy 4:1 states, "Now the Spirit speaketh expressly that in the latter times some shall depart from the faith giving heed to seductive spirits and doctrines of the devil." Doctrines of the devil is anything that goes against what Christ is teaching. Anything that opposes the Word of God is deception. For example, in today's society, we are moved greatly by social media. The internet can be good or bad depending on how we use it. In this post-modern society, we are dealing with seducing spirits, a spirit of error, and the spirit of the antichrist.

Psychology teaches bad behavior can be corrected by your own self-will. Also, the programs are centered around an educated man who may not have an idea what your body, mind and soul is going through. 1st John 3:5 states, "And ye know that he was manifested to take away our sins; and in him is no sin."

The Bible states in 1st John 3:8, "He that committeth sin is of the devil; for the devil sinneth from the beginning. For this purpose, the Son of God was manifested, that he might destroy the works of the devil;" thus we know to eradicate sin through the blood of Jesus

Christ, who is the Great Deliver. Yes, deliverance can only take place through the name and the power of the blood of Jesus Christ. When Jesus died on the cross, he redeemed us from the curse of the law which is bondage. Although we know when we need to be delivered from a compulsive addiction, compulsive addictions cannot be stopped in your human will. Thus, drugs, sex, or even mental addiction issues may not seem to go away at your desire. You may ask, *"How do I get deliverance? Do I really have a problem?"* One of the answers to overcoming strongholds is fasting and praying. Fasting and praying is the oldest effective method for every blood-washed believer. In Matthew 17:21, Jesus addressed the concept of fasting and prayer and taught Peter, James and John saying, "This kind does not go out except by prayer and fasting." The answer to how to overcome challenges and strongholds is fasting and prayer. I use fasting as a strong weapon to attack strongholds in my life. Men and women of the Bible used to fast for different reasons. The Bible also teaches us about different fast through Esther and Daniel to name a few.

Psalm 51:5 states, "I was shaped in iniquity, and in sin did my mother conceive me." You may ask, "*What is iniquity?*" Iniquity is immoral or grossly unfair behavior that destroys your soul, spirit and mind. Because we are born into sin, sin is our natural behavior sometimes being hereditary (generational) because the iniquity has been handed down. Behaviors can be handed down rather it is good behavior or bad behavior. As mentioned previously, this behavior can be corrected through the power of the blood of Jesus Christ.

Psychology is the study of human behavior, mental processes and their effects on an organism's physical state, mental state and external environment. 1st Timothy 4:2 states, *"Speaking lies in hypocrisy; having their conscience seared with a hot iron;"* Did you know that God made your body to heal itself? If you rely on God's power and God's blood, he will heal you. A mind set of wrong thinking can be bondage. There is good mental thinking, and there is bad mental thinking. While Psychology tells us, it is okay to think a certain way, the scripture teaches us different in Romans 12:2, "And be not conformed to this world: but be ye transformed by the renewing of your mind, that ye may prove what is the good, and acceptable, and perfect, will of God. God wants us to be healthy mentally, and to think on good thoughts.

Psychology behavior analysts offer therapy to correct harmful behavior. Psalm 119:105, "Thy word is a lamp unto my feet, and a light unto my path." Because the Word of God is like a light showing you your sins, the scripture reveals how dirty and sinful we actually are! The word also shows God's unmerited grace and mercy! Sinful behavior can be corrected through Psychology but it cannot be cleansed through Psychology. Only the unadulterated word of God because the scripture says *in John* 1:9, "If we confess our sins, he is faithful and just to forgive us our sins, and to cleanse us from all unrighteousness." Our character is formed by the way of our culture, environment, generational inheritance and based on our regional and territorial upbringing. Regardless if acts of sin appear to seem normal, God declares that sin is not exceptional.

Chapter 1

Strongholds
Abnormal Behavior

Who his own self beared our sins in his own body on the tree, that we, being dead to sin should live unto righteousness by whose stripes we are healed.
1 Peter 2:24

Psychopathology is the study of abnormal behavior. *Psychopathology* is a term which refers to the study of mental illness, mental distress, or the manifestation of behaviors and experiences which may be indicative of mental illness or psychological impairment. There are various professions which may be involved in the studying of mental illness, or distress. Abnormal behavior can be treated (psychiatry) clinically but what if medication does not work? Abnormal behavior is a result of the combined and interacting forces of biological, psychological, and social interaction. Let's find the root of abnormal behavior where it originated from learned experiences when abnormal behavior begins. These abnormal behaviors can be unlearned. Our brain is equipped to learn and unlearn things.

Have you ever seen someone who has a mental condition? Perhaps you have been in a circumstance where you felt you suffered from depression, aggressiveness, anger, and the list goes on! There are so many spirits that can weigh on us. There are spirits that can oppress us, and others may possess us. A question that I have often wondered is, *"Do we have power over such spirits?"* The Bible teaches us in Genesis 1:26, "Then God said, *"Let Us make mankind in Our image, according to Our likeness; and let them rule over the fish of the sea and over the birds of the sky and over the livestock and over all the earth, and over every crawling thing that crawls on the earth."* God gave us the power to control everything. In this scripture, God gives mankind which is inclusive of women, boys and girls power. This power is that of the Holy Spirit which can be used to control all things, even abnormal spirits, abnormal behavior and powers of the darkness.

Sometimes our culture causes us to be blind to sin! For example, if we see something so much, our brains can begin to process what is actually abnormal to be normal. Sinful cultures can make sin seem harmless. The practices of certain behaviors or traits are not godly. Sin is always harmful, and when manifested will invite spirits to harm our lives. Generationally, sometimes spirits dwell in familiar places. You may wonder, *"How do we know that we have a stronghold?"* Symptoms of a stronghold are depression, sickness that runs in a family and does not respond to medicine or prayer, uncontrolled desires that you do not want to have. These desires can be lust or any kind of sexual sin. Addiction can be anything such as drugs, sex, alcohol, gambling and even family dysfunctions. If you are confused all of the time, this is a stronghold. Once you realize that your mind is captive with these strongholds, you have to take the following steps to become delivered.

Procedure for Deliverance

- ***Confession.*** For many of us, admitting that we have a stronghold is a challenge. I ask you, *"How can you become free if you do not know that you are bound?"* You cannot be freed of a stronghold until you confess that there is a strong hold over your life. When you confess, ask the Lord to remove the addiction, command it to leave in the Name of Jesus, and through his blood. According to Matthew 18: 18, *"Verily I say unto you, Whatsoever ye shall bind on earth shall be bound in heaven: and whatsoever ye shall lose on earth shall be lose in heaven."* You have to bind the addiction, then lose the Spirit of God over your life. When you bind something, you have to lose something. Lose the spirit of adoption because we have been adopted into the Body of Christ. Lose the spirit of peace, joy and happiness. We should lose the spirit of love. We should lose the Spirit of Truth. You want to lose purity and Holiness. You want to lose according to Isaiah 61:3, the garment of Praise and the oil of joy. You also want to lose the comforter which is the Holy Spirit. You want to lose the Resurrection of our Lord and Savior Jesus Christ.

- **Cast out.** Once you confess it, you cast it out of you and break its power off of you in the name of Jesus. There is power in the name of Jesus. Reminder, always plead the Blood of Jesus over any impure thought. Your name will not be powerful enough to rely on! You have to cast out in the name of Jesus Christ, and in doing so you will become delivered.

- **Command it to leave.** Bind the strongman which is the stronghold; Break every covenant or relationship with the stronghold. Do not continue to be in relationship or in agreement with any spirit that exalts itself against Christ. A covenant is a type of promise and or agreement. However, once you become delivered, you may have to break ties with certain groups or people regardless if it is personal or interpersonal. Philippians 2:5 teaches us, "Let this mind be in you, which was also in Christ Jesus:" Once you command the spirit to leave, stay connected to Christ Jesus.

It starts in the mind.

1) Warfare starts in your mind. Strongholds start in your mind.

2) Wash your mind with the word of God.

3) Your mind needs a mind cleansing.

4) Abnormal behavior or strongholds begins in the mind, repressing thoughts of sinful acts of lust, stealing dangerous acts, drug, alcoholic, sexual appetites that lead to incest, raping, perverse acts. The scripture states in 1st John 3:8, *"For this purpose the son of God was manifested that he might destroy the works of the devil."* Exodus 20:5-6 *"You shall not bow down to them or worship them; for I, the Lord your God, am a jealous*

God, punishing the children for the sin of the parents to the third and fourth generation of those who hate me. And shewing mercy unto thousands of them that love me, and keep my commandments." A stronghold is formed whenever an unclean habit is repeated because your flesh begins to enjoy this unclean habit. Then strongholds become a habit you think is just normal but sooner or later, we crave that habit more than normal. A stronghold has just been formed. A stronghold is an area where Satan is master over you, and you are not the master. A stronghold can be handed down, passed through generational curses, always identifying root causes of the hold that is on you. But Jesus Christ broke the curse according to Galatians 3:13 "Christ hath redeemed us from the curse of the law, being made a curse for us: for it is written, cursed is everyone that hangeth on a tree." A stronghold can develop through one's act of disobedience, rape, and volunteer sinful behavior over and over.

Repetitive sinful behavior indicates there are more than one stronghold in operation. If there is more than one stronghold, it is possible that there is a demonic infestation where a lot of unclean spirits are in operation. There is a demonic infestation of more than one stronghold. Find the root. Pray and ask the spirit of God through discernment to reveal what spirit you are dealing with.

For example, when a baby is born the baby has a lot of stuff on it. We are just like babies because when we come to the Lord, we have a lot of contamination on us from the world. Just like a newborn baby has to be cleaned, we have to be cleaned through the Word of God by praying and fasting. We can come to God despite what sin or contamination we feel we have on us. Whatever the issue is, there is no problem, no addiction, no illness that is too big for God to remove from our lives. God desires to clean us up, and make us whole. Trust and believe.

Chapter 2

Recognizing Victories In Jesus Christ Curses

But he was wounded for our transgressions, he was bruised for our iniquities, the chastisement of our peace was upon him and with his stripes we are healed.

Isaiah 53:5

The definition of sin is to miss the mark. Once the mark has been missed, it should not be normal to continue missing the mark. You may ask yourself, *"What is the mark?"* God gave ten commandments to Moses in Exodus 20:1-17. The purpose of these commandments was intended for humanity to have a mark which a standard to live by. God gave us ten commandments which we should honor; however, we have failed God time and time again. As people, we continue to miss the mark and fall short. God saw early on in Genesis 6:3A, that HIS spirit will not always strive with man. The scripture states, "And the LORD said, My spirit shall not always strive with man, for that he also *is* flesh:" The fact that humans are imperfect, and battle spirits of the darkness has existed since the beginning of time according to the scripture. Sin started in the Garden of Eden when we initially rebelled against God's commandment. While instructed not to sin, Adam and Eve disobeyed God. Jesus Christ was manifested to bring us back to our first glory, and is the perfect Lamb who was slain to bring us back to our original Glory which all started in the Garden of Eden.

Perhaps you have experienced knowing someone whose life seemed to be controlled by darkness as if the light did not exist? Have you ever wondered to yourself, *"How can I get delivered from a spirit that seems to rule and control my life?"* Sin is a spirit. Once we have lived under sin so long (a continuation of disobedience to God's word), we miss the mark ongoing. Sin becomes normal; thus, we become cursed. A curse is a result or disobedience and a continuance of ungodly behavior. Sinful behaviors and habits are actually spirits. Spirits are territorial, and they dwell in familiar places. If you or anyone you may know seems to battle with a spirit that they cannot seem to overcome, they may actually be dealing with a curse. Our society has adopted various dysfunctional behaviors to be normal. Sin is not normal. Curses should not be adopted and considered as normal.

Curses are not only a result of disobedience, but also can occur because of words that are or were spoken. In further detail, if Johnny is a young child, and Johnny's father is alcoholic, some may believe in the saying, *"Like father like son."* However, Johnny does not have to become an alcoholic as a result of his father being one.

The curse can stop! While the curse can end with Johnny's father, if someone is speaking negativity over Johnny, they may be speaking alcoholism into becoming a problem for young Johnny. Saying, *"You will be just like your daddy. You are no better than your father."* These types of words should not be spoken because we do not want them to manifest. The Bible teaches us in Proverbs 18:21, "Life and death are in the power of the tongue." If you notice a struggle in your family, regardless of what it is, be mindful to not let anyone speak negatively over you or your family members. I have heard someone say, *"Something drove me to do a thing."* The question I would ask is, *"What made you do it?"* A spirit or spirits can force people to do certain things.

Romans 8:3 states "God sent his only son to condemn sin in the flesh." Just how we have generational blessings, we also have generational curses. Generational curses could be handed down voluntarily, involuntary, or when we ourselves fabricate and open doors to a stronghold or a foothold. Generational curses could involve drug abuse hand down from generation to generation, spirits of rebellion, sexual sins, idolatry, witchcraft, poverty, mental disorder, dizziness, sickness, disease, continue in strife and family, divorce, or marriage out of wedlock.

A foothold is when you are participating in a sin, and it may control you or your family for years. A stronghold always begins as a foot hole. It is called a foot hole because it comes in through a small door, and little by little, as you open the door someone or that spirit will be able to come in. To sin in continuance is called a spirit. Once it turns into a spirit, it hooks up with other spirits and it becomes an infestation. Your human capacity cannot control it because it is now controlling you. At this stage the stronghold has become the lord in your life. The only cure for this is prayer, and deliverance through Christ our Lord. The Word has to clean us, but you have to seek him. The Word is Jesus Christ!

We do not realize that spirits watch us and are assigned to watch us as we grow. In the spirit world, spirits can watch us and can imitate us. They will watch and oppress us to do the habits of our forefathers. For instance, we have generational curses that are local and regional. They study us and our family. They are waiting for the foothold to recreate that habit that your parents or grandparents had. A foothold is when you allow something to continue to grow in you like how you grow, that will eventually have control over you and or your family. Just as evil spirits of the dark are assigned to watch us, God's Holy Spirit is omnipotent. The Holy Spirit has been with you since and before the day you were born. The Holy Spirit is called the paraclete (meaning comforter) because the Holy Spirit not only watches over you, but also as a mediator for you to God. The Holy Spirit will protect and heal you from all strongholds, sin and diseases the moment you call on the name of Jesus Christ and ask his spirit, the Holy Spirit to fill your soul.

Romans 8:1 state, "There is therefore now no condemnation to them which are in Christ Jesus, who walk not after the flesh, but after the Spirit." Because of Paul's writings, we understand that what the law could not do, Jesus Christ has done. Romans 8:3, *"For what the law could not do, in that it was weak through the flesh, God sending his own Son in the likeness of sinful flesh, and for sin, condemned sin in the flesh:"* The flesh always goes against God. Jesus Christ was manifested that he was destroyed in the flesh. Because of this, your flesh has to submit to God when you call on the name of our Lord, Jesus Christ because the scripture states, "For whosoever shall call upon the name of the Lord shall be saved" (Romans 10:13).

When we crucify our flesh daily, we become sons and daughters. We receive the promises of God. We receive the benefits of the family of Christ because when we become adopted, we become a chosen generation and a royal priesthood. "For if ye live after the flesh, ye shall die: but if ye through the Spirit do mortify the deeds of the body, ye shall live."(Romans 8:13) We have a whole new identity. Old things have passed away. All things become new.

Exodus 34: 6-7, *"And the Lord passed by before him, and proclaimed, The Lord, The Lord God, merciful and gracious, longsuffering, and abundant in goodness and truth, keeping mercy for thousands, forgiving iniquity and transgression and sin, and that will by no means clear the guilty; visiting the iniquity of the fathers upon the children, and upon the children's children, unto the third and to the fourth generation."* In the First Epistle of John, Jesus came to destroy the works of the devil. 1 John 3:8 states, "He who sins is of the devil, for the devil has sinned from the beginning. For this purpose, the Son of God was manifested, that He might destroy the works of the devil." Any acts that are not Biblical or acts that are ungodly should be destroyed in us. We can look at these scriptures how both indicate how generational curses are handed down and manifested if we do not repent and pray.

Possible Curse Or Stronghold

Emotional Instability is when you need help to focus and may have a chemical imbalance.

Mental Instability is when you cannot function properly because you need medication. Mental Instability can be inherited. This disorder can be inherited.

Mentally Depressed

Mental Depression can be inherited. Any disorder can be inherited. People sometimes accept this strong hold and learn to live with it. Do not be around anyone who is depressed all of the time. These spirits live off of each other.

Fear

Fear is an unpleasant emotion that causes traumatic pain, distress or becomes a threat. Fear opposes the **Peace** that God promises us. For this reason, this type of fear is not of God.

There are different types of fears; A person could have a fear of death, a fear of being in front of other people, a fear of rejection, a fear of divorce, a fear of being alone, a fear of what people think or say about you, fear of not being good enough, a fear of change in life.

Hereditary Family Sickness

Some family sickness is reoccurring which means that they are hereditary. These include, but are not limited to, asthma, allergies, lingering disorders, any form of cancer, diabetes, arthritis, heart disease, Leukemia, high blood pressure, Lupus.

Barrenness, Impotence, Female Problems

This is when your body is prone to catching infections even as venereal disease infections. Hormone problems, menstrual problems, PMS Cramps fibroids, painful sex, barrenness, miscarriages, cysts, tumors. Men can also manifest this curse with erectile dysfunction and impotence. This disorder can be inherited.

Family Breakdowns, Divorce, Family divides, Fight Among Relatives, No Fellowship And Families Scatter.

This is separation in the family, and when hate is more prevalent than love. It is not normal every time a family fellowships that a division occurs. This is a curse or a stronghold. God is for the Nuclear Family Structure. The world teaches us to adopt different standards for marriages; however, these are strongholds. Any group that opposes the Nuclear Family is opposing God.

Lack, Poverty, Inability To Produce

The spirit of struggle. The spirit of poverty and struggle are two different spirits. Sometimes a struggle will come, and if the struggle ends another one has come.

- No ambition, vision, or direction
- Bondage and slavery

Spirits Of Infirmity

Etiology is when a sickness or disease is unknown. This is when a person is ill, but the doctors cannot discover the cause or the type of disease it is to diagnose this abnormal condition.

Chapter 3

Identifying Drug And Alcohol Abuse Deliverance From Drug And Alcohol Abuse

> The spirit of the Lord is upon me because the Lord has anointed me to preach the good tidings to the poor. He has sent me to heal the brokenhearted, to proclaim liberty to the captives and the opening of the prion to those who are bound. To proclaim the acceptable year of the Lord.
>
> Isaiah 61:1

Drug abuse is a stronghold that can be broken! For persons who are addicted to drugs, they are actually a slave to the drug. Romans 6:20, *"For when you were slaves of sin, you were free in regard to righteousness;"* Paul teaches us to yield to sin makes us a slave. We should not be a slave to sin; however, there are many things that can cause a person to sin which is drug use. Sometimes people experience hard times, such as, broken marriages, loss of loved ones, broken relationships, peer pressure, curiosity to try something new and to know how it feels, post-traumatic stress disorder (PTSD) are just to name a few. Because of several reasons, people may resort to drugs and alcoholism.

While we should never resort to drugs as a result of hurt, pain or depression, a lot of times these emotions result in drug usage. This is an example of spirit grouping because one spirit attracts another spirit. Spirits of hurt, pain or depression can attract spirits of drug use. Because of the popularity of drugs in our society, it may appear strange to certain people if a person is not using any type of drugs or alcohol. Both drugs and alcohol are spirits, and when using them these spirits gain access to you controlling your thoughts and emotions. You do not have to be tied to the addiction. You can be set free by the renewing of your mind. Romans 12:2 teaches us of transformation in our minds, "And be not conformed to this world: but be ye transformed by the renewing of your mind, that ye may prove what is that good, and acceptable, and perfect, will of God;" Despite what we are opposed with, we should pray to have the mind of Jesus Christ which means to have his thoughts.

Quick Facts on Drug Addiction

- According to the National Survey on Drug Use and Health (NSDUH), 19.7 million American adults (aged 12 and older) battled a substance use disorder in 2017.

- Almost 74% of adults suffering from a substance use disorder in 2017 struggled with an alcohol use disorder.
- About 38% of adults in 2017 battled an illicit drug use disorder.
- That same year, 1 out of every 8 adults struggled with both alcohol and drug use disorders simultaneously.
- In 2017, 8.5 million American adults suffered from both a mental health disorder and a substance use disorder, or co-occurring disorders.
- Drug abuse and addiction cost American society more than $740 billion annually in lost workplace productivity, healthcare expenses, and crime-related costs.

Drug use is among the many types of strongholds we have discussed. If you or anyone you know is struggling with abuse, here are the steps to seeking deliverance.

Steps For Deliverance:

1) Admit that you have an addiction. Forgive yourself for the abuse.
2) Bind the spirit of drug addiction (identify its root). Matthew 18:18 states, "Verily I say unto you, Whatsoever ye shall bind on earth shall be bound in heaven: and whatsoever ye shall lose on earth shall be lose in heaven."
3) Apply the word of God to renew your mind.
4) Confess all known sins or addictions because 1st John 1:9 states, "If we confess our sins, he is faithful and just to forgive us of *our* sins, and to cleanse us from all unrighteousness." After you confess, you have to break off all ties with the addiction such as the places you used to go, and the people you may have known.
5) Apply fasting as a weapon through prayer that helps to kill the addiction. Apply the Blood of Jesus Christ over yourself and claim victory every day.

Remember, deliverance is available to you! Apply fasting as you seek your deliverance.

Alcoholism is a spirit that can transfer from one generation to another. The alcoholic needs to realize they have a problem. Seeking spiritual help and great prayer, deliverance, prayer, warrior and fasting can lessen the desire.

- Admit you are addicted.

- Confess to God that you have a problem.

- Pronounce it.

- Start fasting and allow the Holy Spirit to remove the crave until deliverance come.

- Always have a support group or people of pray to stand in the gap for you.

Chapter 4

Identifying Lust
Deliverance From Lust

For what the law could not do, in that it was weak through the flesh, God sending his own son in the likeness of sinful flesh he condemned sin in the flesh.

Romans 8:3

You are what you think! You are what you allow! Proverbs 23:7 teaches us, "So as a man thinketh in his heart, so is he;" Some things we have to renounce meaning we can reject it. Lust is a spirit that is territorial and generational. While you may not have wanted to be born into a family with certain spirits, you can be delivered from these strongholds. There are several types of lust, and all are sinful. Acts that derive from lust is molestation (child abuse), rape, adultery (unfaithfulness in marriage), same sex relationships, and even fornication.

Proverbs 18:21 states, "Life and death is in the power of the tongue." Whatever you speak you overcome. If you speak down on yourself, you will be down. If you speak life and blessings to yourself, you will have such. Always speak life over yourself if you have been a victim of lust. The Devil's job is to destroy us, as mentioned in 1st Peter 5:8, "Be sober, be vigilant; because your adversary, the devil, as a roaring lion, walketh about, seeking whom he may devour." Satan will attempt to destroy families and generations through the strongholds of lust.

The spirit of lust can be passed down generationally, our own involvement or those being violated. Sexual bondage is strong! The only way to conquer sexual sin is through the renewing of our mind through the scriptures. It takes changing your life and applying the word. Whenever holds are strong, I personally recommend fast. It is the most effective tool for someone who is anointed by God to cast the unclean spirit out. This stronghold can destroy a person, family, and even a great Man of God. Far too often in our society and world great leaders, great educators, great parents and great people in general are destroyed because of their acts due to the strongholds of lust.

All throughout the Bible, we can read where God came down on His people when it came to idolatry and sexual sins. You may ask, *"Why?"* The reason why is because we share ourselves with God. He should be the only lover of our soul. God desires to be one with you so much, that he sent his only son Jesus Christ to die on the cross (John 3:16). After the resurrection of Christ our Lord, he left his Holy Spirit (a piece of him) here on Earth with us, so that we can always be one with him. In John 14:16, Jesus explains, "But the Comforter, *which is* the

Holy Ghost, whom the Father will send in my name, he shall teach you all things, and bring all things to your remembrance, whatsoever I have said unto you." Lust opposes the Spirit of God, and anyone who acts in such manner is not of God.

Steps To Deliverance:

1) Confess to yourself that you have lust issues.
2) Renounce it. This means to reject, and rebuke it. Be determined not to pass this demonic spirit or stronghold to anyone else. Break all spirits associated with the lust spirit.
3) Go on a fast that will decrease the temptation or getting the spirit cast out.
4) Allow the Holy Ghost to tell you which fast to go on.

Whenever these thoughts come to your mind, remember to cast down the thought. 2nd Corinthians 10:5, "Casting down imaginations, and every high thing that exalteth itself against the knowledge of God, and bringing into captivity every thought to the obedience of Christ." Everyday continue to thank Jesus Christ for deliverance and for setting you free. The more you thank him, the more he will deliver.

Chapter 5

Identifying Slothfulness Deliverance From Slothfulness

Whatsoever you do, do it heartily as to the lord and not unto man.

Colossians 3:23

Not slothful in business, frequent in spirit and serving the Lord.

Romans 12:11

Slothfulness is a spirit. Procrastination is a spirit. Because of slothfulness, a person may procrastinate or even tell a lie as far as why the work or task was not completed. Interesting excuses can become addictive. Not moving in God's timing can be disobedience. If God speaks to you and tells you to do something, but you do not do it, this is disobedience which may cause you to miss something. The scripture states to reach for the mark of the higher calling which is in our Lord Christ Jesus; however, slothfulness will cause us to miss the mark. In Christ, it matters what we are doing. It is better to do something than not to do anything.

God wants us to be working! If you are living in your purpose, you should never have an absent moment. While many of today's Christians are sluggish, we should not be. Laziness is not only a stronghold, but it is a stronghold that God himself despises. For example, the Bible states in 1 Timothy 5:8, "Anyone who does not provide for their relatives, and especially for their own household, has denied the faith and is worse than an unbeliever." We should work. We should want to work. God appreciates our labor.

Whenever we fail to listen to God's voice, we will lose out and suffer. Do you recall when the Prophet Elisha told Naaman to go dip himself in the Jordan River seven times? Naaman was a mighty man of valor, but he had leprosy. Naaman procrastinated because he could not figure out why a man of such high stature should go to the Jordan River being that the Jordan was one of the most unclean rivers. However, once Naaman's handmaiden servant spoke to him to go, he eventually went. Had not Naaman gone, he would not have been made whole. The idea is that when God speaks, we must not delay; however, we must move forward and with haste! 2nd Kings 5:27 states, Naaman's leprosy will cling to you and to your descendants forever." Then Gehazi went from Elisha's presence and his skin was leprous—it had become as white as snow." Although Naaman was upset and did not want to go down to Jordan, he was cleansed once he did what the Prophet told him to do.

Sometimes we like to blame circumstances in our lives, when we are the blame. Always remember, that slothfulness is a spirit which creates a stronghold, and this is not of God. Romans 8:3, "For what the law could not do, in that it was weak through the flesh, God sent his own Son in the likeness of sinful flesh, and for sin, condemned sin in the flesh." You have to apply God's word. This is the process that will set us free! You have to feed yourself the Word of God. A lot of people want an easy fix. We are a microwave generation! Sometimes being in Christ is tough. It is not always easy doing what God wants us to do, or like Naaman, what the Prophet has told us to do. We have to get up and obey as service to God requires work. Slothfulness can easily be declined as laziness as the Bible states Proverbs 13:4; "A sluggard's appetite is never filled, but the desires of the diligent are fully satisfied."

We can see all of these things as leprosy because it is an unwanted condition. However, we cannot rid ourselves of these illnesses! Do not try to fix yourself. Call on the name of Jesus and ask him to fix you. Colossians 3:23; "Whatever you do, work at it with all your heart, as working for the Lord, not for human masters." This scripture allows us to know that we should not only work, but also work diligently meaning that our heart should be connected to our work. This scripture alone is powerful because our heart connects to our purpose in life. If we are lazy, we will miss out on our purpose.

2 Thessalonians 3:10 states, "For even when we were with you, we gave you this rule: The one who is unwilling to work shall not eat." Clearly, the Bible teaches us that slothfulness is a sin. Slothfulness only produces failure. Slothfulness is one of the seven deadly sins.

How To Conquer Slothfulness

1) Confess to God that you are an individual who does not complete things, and why you make excuses why you have not completed certain tasks. Confess to God that you often start tasks, and do not finish them.

2) Renounce the spirit of laziness and sluggardness. Declare that you will not accept this over your life. Continue to tell yourself that I am complete in Christ. Rebuke the spirit of laziness and being sluggard, so that it will not have dominion over you.

3) Break its powers by binding the spirit of slothfulness, and release the spirit of liberty.

4) Claim victory by saying, *"Thank Jesus I am more than a conqueror. I am spiritually and wonderfully made. I am filled with the promises of God. I am an overcomer and I am complete in Jesus Christ! I am the apple of my father's eyes."*

Chapter 6

Identifying Generational Curses Deliverance From Generational Curses

If the son therefore shall make you free, you shall be free indeed.

John 8:36

A generational curse is a stronghold that has traveled from one generation to the next. Matthew 12:43 states, "When an impure spirit comes out of a person, it goes through arid places seeking rest and does not find it." Spirits search for a dwelling place. Because of this, it is important that Believers continuously pray, and rebuke evil. All strongholds are evil. Any generational curse is evil. Strongholds can be passed from your parents, grandparents and even other members of your family. Exodus 20:5-6 states, "Thou shalt not bow down thyself to them, nor serve them: for I the Lord thy God am a jealous God, visiting the iniquity of the fathers upon the children unto the third and fourth generation of them that hate me; And shewing mercy unto thousands of them that love me, and keep my commandments." These types of strongholds can hurt, as you do not want to recognize them in the people you love. Various types of illnesses can be passed on as a generational curse. Jesus Christ demolished sin 1 John 3:5:8, manifested that he may take away our sins and destroy every curse.

If you recognize a generational curse in your family, deliverance comes through fasting, praying and working to overcome. Sometimes in a grace movement, people may think that they are saved because they go to church, and that deliverance comes by their church attendance. However, going to church does not mean that you are delivered. Deliverance is for the believer if the believer applies the Word of God. Application of the Word of God brings healing, and wholeness. While we may preach grace, we should not omit holiness. When God completed the finish work on the cross, he told us to imitate him. Jesus Christ said, "Let this mind that was also in Christ Jesus be in you." It is important that we fight our spiritual warfare in the Spirit of Christ Jesus.

Just because society or our postmodern world says that something is right does not mean that it is right. Deliverance from generational curse and territorial curse. You can pass on biological habits, physical traits, health, poverty, wealth, and environmental hereby through family lineage that can affect the body, soul and mind but also, we can cancel generational curses handed down by applying the word of God and blood of Jesus.

How To Overcome Generational Curses

- Admit to God that there is a problem. Say, *"Lord, this is a problem in my family."*

- Renounce all generational curse.

- Ask God to cleanse and separate you from the curses through his blood that he atoned on the cross. Believe that he has already cleansed you through his atonement.

- Cancel every assignment of struggling. Bind it in the name of Jesus according to Matthew 18:8.

- Lose it and cancel every assignment.

- Release the spirit of God, liberty, purity, prosperity, and wholeness in your family in Jesus' name.

Diabetes, high blood pressure and poverty are all types of strongholds placed over families that can become generational curses. If your family struggles with poverty, start tithing and giving. If diabetes or high blood pressure is a stronghold in your family, eat healthy, drink lots of water and exercise. Jesus Christ is the ultimate model role to follow. You may see a celebrity on television, and think to yourself, *"Oh, I want to be like them!"* But you do not know what their struggles are. 3 John 1:2, KJV: "Beloved, I wish above all things that thou mayest prosper and be in health, even as thy soul prospereth." It is evident in this scripture that God wants us to be in good health and he wants us to be financially prosperous as well.

Chapter 7

The Power Of God's Word Healing Power

Now ye are cleaned through the word which I have spoken unto you.

John 15:3

Never speak negative words over yourself! Always speak life. Encourage yourself even when life tends to discourage you. Say, *"Lord, I am righteous."* Whenever sin tries to surround you, seek the manifestation of the Holy Spirit. Declare and say out loud, *"I am more than a conqueror."* Once you have made these declarations, go forward and act on it. Act as if you are more than a conqueror, and you will be victorious over sin and strongholds. Declare and decree that you are delivered! Whenever the stronghold, past sin or even generational curses try to disrupt your lifestyle, believe in the healing power of God's Word. Because the Word of God provides deliverance from sin and strongholds, healing and wellness, the Devil tries to make the scriptures a blur to us. Did you know that when Jesus Christ was tempted in the wilderness by Satan, Jesus spoke the word.

Matthew 4: 1-11

Then Jesus was led by the Spirit into the wilderness to be tempted by the devil. **2** After fasting forty days and forty nights, he was hungry. **3** The tempter came to him and said, "If you are the Son of God, tell these stones to become bread."

4 Jesus answered, "It is written: 'Man shall not live on bread alone, but on every word that comes from the mouth of God.

5 Then the devil took him to the holy city and had him stand on the highest point of the temple. **6** "If you are the Son of God," he said, "throw yourself down. For it is written:

"'He will command his angels concerning you,

and they will lift you up in their hands,

so that you will not strike your foot against a stone.

7 Jesus answered him, "It is also written: 'Do not put the Lord your God to the test.

8 Again, the devil took him to a very high mountain and showed him all the kingdoms of the world and their splendor. **9** "All this I will give you," he said, "if you will bow down and worship me."

10 Jesus said to him, "Away from me, Satan! For it is written: 'Worship the Lord your God, and serve him only.

11 Then the devil left him, and angels came and attended him.

Just as Satan attempted to trick Jesus, Satan will try to cause us to sin, experience generational curses or even live with strongholds. You must know that sin is never God's will. If you do not know the Word of God, you will not be able to fight the Devil. I encourage you to learn the scriptures; Know the Word of God. Psalm 119:11 states, "Your word I have hidden in my heart, That I might not sin against You." We also learn the importance of the Word of God when the scripture states previously, in Psalm 119:10 "With all my heart I have sought You; do not let me stray from Your commandments." God's Word is not only important but also a necessity for the survival of the believer. God's Holy Scriptures are the only way that we would rid ourselves of these evils.

Did you know that a Proverb means a wise saying? The book of Proverbs is filled with wisdom that can enrich and heal us from a life of malfunction and discourse. Proverb 18:21 states, "Death and life are in the power of the tongue and those who love it will eat its fruit." While words can harm you because your soul may believe the lies of Satan, God's Word will sustain you. The word according to James 3:1-11 by word of faith. If you want to be healed, always rely on the Power of God's Word!

Chapter 8
How To Dismiss Addiction & Stronghold
Confess Your Sin

For what the law could not do. It was weak through the flesh, God did by sending his own son in the likeness of sinful flesh, on the account of sin he condemned sin in the flesh that the righteousness requirement of the law might be fulfilled in us who do not walk according to the flesh but according to the spirit.

Romans 8:3-4

In today's postmodern society, there seems to be a thin line between right and wrong. For example, *Christians* are sometimes easily offended by the Word of God when the scriptures should be for the upbuilding of God's Kingdom. While this is so, the Bible actually warned us in Matthew 24:4 "For there shall arise false Christs, and false prophets, and shall shew great signs and wonders; insomuch that, if it were possible, they shall deceive the very elect." We see so many spirits which are strange because these types of sin and spirits are new to us. While immorality has increased like never before, television (media) makes all lifestyles acceptable. But is it acceptable to God? You do not have to be saved to acknowledge wrong. You know deep inside when you are doing something wrong, it is a God given instinct. But we suppress or override this instinct to do what we want to do which is sin.

A spirit will have you believing the lies of Satan. God can deliver you from same-sex relationships, drug addiction, alcohol abuse, sluggardness and whatever strongholds you may be experiencing. As mentioned earlier, you have to seek God, fast and pray to overcome.

Strongholds are never easy to overcome. As a matter of fact, strongholds are always challenging to overcome. God will forgive you of your sins. The following are steps to equip you to overcome. Pray and follow these steps:

1. Reject the thought. Reject the source (Satan).

2. Cast down imagination and every high thing that exalts itself against the Word of God. We have to reject bad sinful thoughts that oppose God.

3. Repent and confess your sin. 1st John 1:9; "If we confess our sins, he is faithful and just and will forgive us of our sins and purify us from all unrighteousness."

4. Claim victory through the Blood of Jesus. Rev 12:11, "And they overcame him by the blood of the Lamb, and by the word of their testimony; and they loved not their lives unto the death." 1st Peter 1:18-19, "For you know that it was not with perishable things such as silver or gold that you were redeemed from the empty way of life handed down to you from

your ancestors, but with the precious blood of Christ, a lamb without blemish or defect."

5. Cry out to God, and ask him to deliver you from your thoughts. Tell God the thoughts that you have. 2nd Corinthians 10: 4-5, "The weapons we fight with are not the weapons of the world. On the contrary, they have divine power to demolish strongholds. We demolish arguments and every pretension that sets itself up against the knowledge of God, and we take captive of every thought to make it obedient to Christ."

6. Fasting is a way of expressing to God that you need healing. Mark 9:20; "So they brought him. When the spirit saw Jesus, it immediately threw the boy into a convulsion. He fell to the ground and rolled around, foaming at the mouth." This scripture is about deliverance. Fasting is one of the most effective ancient methods of seeking and getting deliverance. You can get delivered if you call on the matchless name of Jesus.

Chapter 9

Personal Deliverance & Victory Examples Of Spirits

But thank be to God, which gives the victory through our Lord Jesus Christ.
1st Corinthians 15:57

My personal deliverance and victory came when I first gave my life to Jesus Christ! This was the turning point for me. I was lost and I had no identity. Once I accepted the Lord as my personal savior, my spiritual eyes were opened to the strongholds in my life. Previously, I never saw that I failed to complete tasks, I could not function properly, and I always wondered about who I was. Whenever certain events would take place in my life, I would wonder, *"Why couldn't I overcome them?"* I suffered from depression. Then I realized that my dad, myself and my daughter suffered from depression (this is three generations). I could not understand. Once I realized this, I began to realize that different families suffer from different things. For example, I had a girlfriend who became an alcoholic, and her dad was also an alcoholic. I started realizing more as I began working with people. A lot of spirits were generational with myself and other people.

How sweet was the moment, my eyes were open! My experience reminds me of Amazing Grace; this familiar hymn by John Newton states, *"Amazing grace! How sweet the sound that saved a wretch like me! I once was lost, but now am found; Was blind, but now I see."* While my eyes seemed to have been closed to the various strongholds in my life, I began to see my faults after I accepted Jesus Christ in my life. Deliverance is free, and it is available to you! Romans 2:11 states, "For there is no respect of persons with God." You may wonder, *"What does this scripture mean?"* It means what God has done for one, he will do for you as well. If God can deliver me of the strongholds, sin and generational curses over my life, I know, he can and will do the same for you! Deliverance can happen progressively or instantly. For me, I have experienced when someone laid hands on me, and cast the spirit away (instantaneously), and I have experienced progressive deliverance. Progressive deliverance is when you work towards being Holy, and we have to always remember that because of Christ we are already delivered through faith in our Lord. It is when you cry out daily to God confessing your sins and seeking his help. Regardless if deliverance is instantly or progressively, we should all work daily to overcome any spirit that is not like God.

In your personal walk with God, it is important to pray without ceasing. While you are not intentionally seeking out evil, the Devil is seeking you. Keep your spiritual eyes open and be attentive. 1 Peter 5:8 reminds us, *"Be sober, be vigilant; because your adversary the devil, as a roaring lion, walks about, seeking whom he may devour."* You may even recall in Job 1:7 the conversation that the Lord had with the Devil, *"And the LORD said unto Satan, Whence comest thou? Then Satan answered the LORD, and said, from going to and fro in the earth, and from walking up and down in it."* Satan is on a mission and he is seeking to destroy you. Be aware and be prayerful!

Ephesians 6:10-18 KJV

"Finally, my brethren, be strong in the Lord, and in the power of his might. Put on the whole armor of God, that ye may be able to stand against the wiles of the devil. For we wrestle not against flesh and blood, but against principalities, against powers, against the rulers of the darkness of this world, against spiritual wickedness in high places. Wherefore take unto you the whole armor of God, that ye may be able to withstand in the evil day, and having done all, to stand. Stand therefore, having your loins girt

about with truth, and having on the breastplate of righteousness; And your feet shod with the preparation of the gospel of peace; Above all, taking the shield of faith, wherewith ye shall be able to quench all the fiery darts of the wicked. And take the helmet of salvation, and the sword of the Spirit, which is the word of God: Praying always with all prayer and supplication in the Spirit, and watching thereunto with all perseverance and supplication for all saints."

Chapter 10

Scriptures Of Deliverance & Healing The Power Of Fasting And Prayer

For the weapons of our warfare are not carnal but mighty in God for pulling down strongholds, casting down arguments and every high thing that exalts itself against the knowledge of God, bringing every thought into captivity to the obedience of Christ.

2 Corinthians 10:4-5

Scriptures On Deliverance

The righteous cry, and the Lord heareth, and delivered them out of all their troubles.

Psalm 34:17

If ye abide in me, and my words abide in you, ye shall ask what ye will, and it shall be done unto you.

John 15:7

For sin shall not have dominion over you: for ye are not under the law, but under grace. What then? shall we sin, because we are not under the law, but under grace? God forbid. Know ye not, that to whom ye yield yourselves servants to obey, his servants ye are to whom ye obey; whether of sin unto death, or of obedience unto righteousness? But God be thanked, that ye were the servants of sin, but ye have obeyed from the heart that form of doctrine which was delivered you. Being then made free from sin, ye became the servants of righteousness. I speak after the manner of men because of the infirmity of your flesh: for as ye have yielded your members servants to uncleanness and to iniquity unto iniquity; even so now yield your members servants to righteousness unto holiness.

Romans 6:14-19

And ye shall know the truth, and the truth shall make you free.

John 8:32

Stand fast therefore in the liberty wherewith Christ hath made us free, and be not entangled again with the yoke of bondage.

Galatians 5:1

Confess your faults one to another, and pray one for another, that ye may be healed. The effectual fervent prayer of a righteous man availed much.

James 5:16

I sought the Lord, and he heard me, and delivered me from all my fears.

Psalm 34:4

And he said, The Lord is my rock, and my fortress, and my deliverer; 3 The God of my rock; in him will I trust: he is my shield, and the horn of my salvation, my high tower, and my refuge, my savior; thou save me from violence.

2 Samuel 22:2-3

And call upon me in the day of trouble: I will deliver thee, and thou shalt glorify me.

Psalm 50:15

Then they cried unto the Lord in their trouble, and he delivered them out of their distresses.

Psalm 107:6

The Lord knoweth how to deliver the godly out of temptations, and to reserve the unjust unto the day of judgment to be punished:

2 Peter 2:9

But the LORD said unto me, Say not, I am a child: for thou shalt go to all that I shall send thee, and whatsoever I command thee thou shalt speak. 8 Be not afraid of their faces: for I am with thee to deliver thee, saith the LORD. 9 Then the LORD put forth his hand, and touched my mouth.

Jeremiah 1:7-9

And I will restore to you the years that the locust hath eaten, the cankerworm, and the caterpillar, and the palmerworm, my great army which I sent among you. And ye shall eat in plenty, and be satisfied, and praise the name of the Lord your God, that hath dealt wondrously with you: and my people shall never be ashamed. And ye shall know that I am in the midst of

Israel, and that I am the Lord your God, and none else: and my people shall never be ashamed.

Joel 2:25-27

Be pleased, O Lord, to deliver me: O Lord, make haste to help me.

Psalm 40:13

But I am poor and needy; yet the Lord thinketh upon me: thou art my help and my deliverer; make no tarrying, O my God

Psalm 40:17

And when he had called unto him his twelve disciples, he gave them power against unclean spirits, to cast them out, and to heal all manner of sickness and all manner of disease.

Matthew 10:1

Scriptures On Healing

But he was wounded for our transgressions, he was bruised for our iniquities: the chastisement of our peace was upon him; and with his stripes we are healed.

Isaiah 53:5

Confess your faults one to another, and pray one for another, that ye may be healed. The effectual fervent prayer of a righteous man availeth much.

James 5:16

"Beloved, I wish above all things that thou mayest prosper and be in health, even as thy soul prospereth."

3 John 1:2

Is any sick among you? let him call for the elders of the church; and let them pray over him, anointing him with oil in the name of the Lord:

James 5:14

Confess your faults one to another, and pray one for another, that ye may be healed. The effectual fervent prayer of a righteous man avails much.

James 5:15-16

Again, I say unto you, That if two of you shall agree on earth as touching anything that they shall ask, it shall be done for them of my Father which is in heaven.

Matthew 18:19

Be careful for nothing; but in everything by prayer and supplication with thanksgiving let your requests be made known unto God.

Philippians 4:6

And Jesus looking upon them saith, with men it is impossible, but not with God: for with God all things are possible.

Mark 10:27

And the prayer of faith shall save the sick, and the Lord shall raise him up; and if he have committed sins, they shall be forgiven him.

James 5:15

Verily, verily, I say unto you, He that believeth on me, the works that I do shall he do also; and greater works than these shall he do; because I go unto my Father.

John 14:12

He sent his word, and healed them, and delivered them from their destructions.

Psalm 107:20

To another faith by the same Spirit; to another the gifts of healing by the same Spirit.

1 Corinthians 12:9

And when ye stand praying, forgive, if ye have ought against any: that your Father also which is in heaven may forgive you your trespasses.

Mark 11:25

If we confess our sins, he is faithful and just to forgive us our sins, and to cleanse us from all unrighteousness.

1 John 1:9

That which is born of the flesh is flesh; and that which is born of the Spirit is spirit.

John 3:6

Blessed is he that considers the poor: the Lord will deliver him in time of trouble. The Lord will preserve him, and keep him alive; and he shall be blessed upon the earth: and thou wilt not deliver him unto the will of his enemies. The Lord will strengthen him upon the bed of languishing: thou wilt make all his bed in his sickness.

Psalm 41:1-3

Above all, taking the shield of faith, wherewith ye shall be able to quench all the fiery darts of the wicked.

Ephesians 6:16

Submit yourselves therefore to God. Resist the devil, and he will flee from you.

James 4:7

14 Is any sick among you? let him call for the elders of the church; and let them pray over him, anointing him with oil in the name of the Lord: 15 And the prayer of faith shall save the sick, and the Lord shall raise him up; and if he has committed sins, they shall be forgiven him.

James 5: 14-15

And said, If thou wilt diligently hearken to the voice of the Lord thy God, and wilt do that which is right in his sight, and wilt give ear to his commandments, and keep all his statutes, I will put none of these diseases upon thee, which I have brought upon the Egyptians: for I am the Lord that healeth thee.

Exodus 15:26

And when he had called unto him his twelve disciples, he gave them power against unclean spirits, to cast them out, and to heal all manner of sickness and all manner of disease.

Matthew 10:1

"They shall take up serpents; and if they drink any deadly thing, it shall not hurt them; they shall lay hands on the sick, and they shall recover."

Mark 16:18

That it might be fulfilled which was spoken by Esaias the prophet, saying, Himself took our infirmities, and bare our sicknesses.

Matthew 8:17

How God anointed Jesus of Nazareth with the Holy Ghost and with power: who went about doing good, and healing all that were oppressed of the devil; for God was with him.

Acts 10:38

Who his own self bare our sins in his own body on the tree, that we, being dead to sins, should live unto righteousness: by whose stripes ye were healed.

1st Peter 2:24

Verily, verily, I say unto you, He that believeth on me, the works that I do shall he do also; and greater works than these shall he do; because I go unto my Father.

John 14:12

You may wonder, *"Why do we fast?"* There are various reasons or purposes to fast. Fasting is to go an intermittent amount of time without essentials, such as: food, water or something we love to the point where we feel we need it. Fasting a form of a sacrifice that we can use to show God, we need him. Fasting is an action that go beyond our verbal prayers. We fast for the power of God in our ministry and in our personal lives. We fast for revelation and understanding of God's Word. We fast for God's Holy Spirit to be manifested. Sometimes we may fast to end a crisis, or an issue going on in our life. We may fast for protection and direction. We may fast for intimacy with God (to be close to him). We can fast for healing, and wholeness in our body, soul and mind. We may fast for the *Shekinah Glory* of God. We may fast for contentment, restoration and strength to go through certain circumstances in life. We may fast for God to raise the next generation and for them to live in God's will and for God's Glory. Regardless of the reason that you may fast, fasting is one of the oldest and effective methods to getting God to answer your prayer.

During a **one day fast,** some people may require water; however, the fast may consist of water or no water. During this fast, read your Bible and pray. Do not eat any food during this fast. A **half day fast** from 6:00 A.M. to 6:00 P.M., do not eat any food during this fast. Paul did a **three day fast** after his conversion in the book of Acts. Read, pray, and keep your petition lifted before the Lord. There are different ways that you can do this fast. Some people do not eat any food at all, while others may eat only vegetables. Esther also fasted for **three days and three nights.** This was a **unity fast** because she was in a specific crisis (Esther 4:16). Daniel fasted **a three week fast** in Daniel 10:2-3. Daniel was fasting for understanding. Jesus and Moses did a **forty day fast**. David fasted **seven days** before his child died. Ezra 8:21-23 **fasted** to seek God's protection. Paul always fasted. Paul fasted to receive prophetic direction. Paul and his team fasted to commission the elders. (Acts

13:14) The church fasted and prayed for Peter to be delivered from prison (Acts 12:1-19).

If you are a Christian, and you want to begin fasting, ask your physician. Depending on your health background, you may want to seek guidance on how you fast. In the morning, pray to position yourself to conquer habits. Read scriptures of healing and deliverance while fasting. Pray scriptures over your habit and addiction! Quote scriptures such as, 2 Timothy 1:7, "For God has not given me the spirit of fear but love, power and of sound mind." Pray to gain soundness is in your mind right now. Pray in the name of Jesus, and you will overcome any battles by the precious blood. You will notice that the stronghold will become less strong and powerless over you.

"*Is* this not the fast that I have chosen:

To lose the bonds of wickedness,

To undo the heavy burdens,

To let the oppressed, go free,

And that you break every yoke?

Is it not to share your bread with the hungry,

And that you bring to your house the poor who are cast out;

When you see the naked, that you cover him,

And not hide yourself from your own flesh?

Then your light shall break forth like the morning,

Your healing shall spring forth speedily,

And your righteousness shall go before you;

The glory of the Lord shall be your rear guard.

Then you shall call, and the Lord will answer;

You shall cry, and He will say, 'Here I *am*.'

"If you take away the yoke from your midst,

The pointing of the finger, and speaking wickedness,

If you extend your soul to the hungry

And satisfy the afflicted soul,

Then your light shall dawn in the darkness,

And your darkness shall *be* as the noonday.

The Lord will guide you continually,

And satisfy your soul in drought,

And strengthen your bones;

You shall be like a watered garden,

And like a spring of water, whose waters do not fail.

Those from among you

Shall build the old waste places;

You shall raise up the foundations of many generations;

And you shall be called the Repairer of the Breach,

The Restorer of Streets to Dwell In."

Isaiah 58:6-13

www.ingramcontent.com/pod-product-compliance
Lightning Source LLC
LaVergne TN
LVHW051849080426
835512LV00018B/3157